NIGHT WING OVER METROPOLITAN AREA

BOOKS BY JOHN HOPPENTHALER

Lives of Water
Anticipate the Coming Reservoir
Domestic Garden
Night Wing over Metropolitan Area

Jean Valentine: This-World Company, co-edited with Kazim Ali

NIGHT WING OVER METROPOLITAN AREA

JOHN HOPPENTHALER

Carnegie Mellon University Press
Pittsburgh 2023

ACKNOWLEDGMENTS

I'm grateful to the editors of the following publications in which these poems, sometimes in different versions, first appeared:

Appalachian Lit: "At 2 a.m."
Asheville Poetry Review: "Happy Hour at Joey Roma's Restaurant and Bar" and "OCD"
Birmingham Poetry Review: "Bourbon, Cigarettes, Van Morrison"
Border Crossing: "Cape Breton Highlands," "Shrine," and "To the Bone"
Chautauqua: "After Listening to the Weather, I Pull into a Bar," "Mitchelville, SC" and "Single Life with Cardinal and American Goldfinch"
Live Encounters: "After Motherwell's Two Figures," "First Light," and "Hummingbirds and Eagles"
Gargoyle: "The Venus of Willendorf"
Great River Review: "Best Friends" and "Superstition"
The Greensboro Review: "The Nature of Nature"
Inkwell: "Current Events"
James Dickey Review: "The Tiniest Toad in Moore County, NC"
Kestrel: "My Second Spring"
Laurel Review: "Chant" and "One Week before the Solstice"
Ocean State Review: "Bird Riff"
One: "Grotto Spring"
Plume: "Nocturne"
Poetry Miscellany: "Chimes"
Poetry Northwest: "Your Daydreaming Child"
South Dakota Review: "Great Again"
Stone Canoe: "Jesus. Frankenstein. Danny's Monsters"
storySouth: "Southern Pines, July 2019"
Valparaiso Poetry Review: "Eureka Springs"

"Night Wing over Metropolitan Area" appears in *You Are the River*, North Carolina Museum of Art Press 2021. "The Tiniest Toad in Moore County, NC" was reprinted in *A Constellation of Kisses*, Terrapin Books 2019. "Chimes" was reprinted in *Redux* 2015. "One among millions" was chosen to be displayed at a variety of sites in Newton, Massachusetts, as part of Poetry Newton's Haiku Newton project, sponsored by the Newton Cultural Council, Massachusetts Cultural Council, and Newton Community Pride 2022.

I want to thank my wife and stepson for their love and perseverance. Thanks to Michael Waters, Mihaela Moscaliuc, Natasha Trethewey, Jim Harms, and Renée Nicholson for their ongoing friendship and support; and special thanks to Jim Harms and Michael Waters for providing critical advice during the manuscript's final stages. As always, thanks to Jerry Costanzo, Cynthia Lamb, Connie Amoroso, and the rest of the Carnegie Mellon University Press staff. I'm grateful to the Weymouth Center for the Humanities, the Virginia Center for the Creative Arts, and the Writers' Colony at Dairy Hollow for residency fellowships during which most of these poems were written or revised. Thank you to Rosanne Cash, Brian Turner and Barbara Hamby for their kind words. Thanks to Michael Paul Thomas for, once again, supplying the headshot. I'm grateful to East Carolina University's Thomas Harriot College of Arts and Sciences for providing a Reassignment Award, and to the East Carolina University Department of English for financial support that made the residencies possible. Thanks to the North Carolina Museum of Art for providing the cover image, and to the D C Moore Gallery for permission to use it at no charge.

Cover art: Yvonne Jacquette, *Night Wing: Metropolitan Area Composite II*, 1993, Oil on canvas, 80 5/8 x 56 ¾ in. North Carolina Museum of Art. Purchased with funds from the North Carolina State Art Society (Robert F. Phifer Bequest). Courtesy of the artist and D C Moore Gallery, New York.

Library of Congress Control Number 2023933222
ISBN 978-0-88748-692-0

10 9 8 7 6 5 4 3 2 1

for my mother, Maria Hoppenthaler
October 28, 1936 – September 9, 2021

CONTENTS

. . . and they brought unto him all sick people that were taken with divers diseases and torments, and those which were possessed with devils, and those which were lunatick, and those that had the palsy; and he healed them.

—Matthew 4:24

It's the same story the crow told me
It's the only one he know
Like the morning sun you come
And like the wind you go

—Jerry Garcia and Robert Hunter

NIGHT WING OVER METROPOLITAN AREA

after Yvonne Helene Jacquette

Wing of a blackbird, wing
of a crow. If I seem a vulture
sometimes, on the wing, adrift

toward carrion, indistinct architecture
of loss, its ambience. . . . The hydraulic
whine and thud of the landing gear, absence

of towers, moderate tremor of shear
and turbulence. No, not buildings, only
insistent light that props them up; their

corporeal bodies dissolved—enormous
emptiness, which itself is full of color, ghosts
of light beyond emptiness, that which defines them,

that which looms outside the frame, space
between us, the pregnant darkness of our
city, and a million tiny votives that oppose.

The night wing hangs, sags toward you with
gravity, weight of a thousand corpses, screech
of a virus, that shrill hawk as I circle

in a holding pattern, and all I can see is
primary color, pointillism of what's left
behind or flown toward, fugitive colors,

especially the blue rims of your eyes. I lift
or descend, and it seems the same: proximity
may as well be absence; arrival means another

place has been left behind, and I'm taking
off or landing to deliver what support I can.
We are two dark birds, together, keeping

raptors at bay—there, out over the river.

I.

FIRST LIGHT

My old nemesis the blue jay
flits down to bathe in the fake pool,
the fake origin of the cool
but fake waterfall. Fake but, hey,
it helps on this hot July day.

We all love to rest in gardens,
which are only reclamations,
human hands remaking Eden.
The bird is washing away sin
as I mope about my burdens.

On coming home late from the bar,
I'd strip near my mother's garden,
pile the smoky clothes as lived in,
stale gift at my parents' back door,
before taking to bed, before
dad's creaking steps toward the bathroom.

The Gospels differ on the tomb,
what Mary saw, whom she met.
The jay's returned, his head turned west.
Assume what you want to assume.

The bird's neck swivels
before he dips his beak down.
The fake font gurgles.

Lifting, an angel
burst of blue into sky blue.
The frog croaks amen.

BEST FRIENDS

Stretched through the narrow canyon of side yards,
bedroom window to bedroom window, between
oak limbs and over their parents' small gardens—
herbs on one side, flowers on the other—nylon string

allows two girls to speak into soup cans and wish
each other good night. It's summer, so daylight lingers,
gray and sad, in mottled skies beyond the ridge.
They could hear the words better if they called out loud.

A starling shakes itself dry on the lip of the birdbath,
and in one of the similar houses, the parents are already
drunk. One child's cat feigns interest for a moment
but soon goes back to sniffing at the chives and parsley.

By the time the Anderson boy roars by—too fast—
on his Yamaha, the two friends have nearly fallen
asleep. The parents who are not loaded remember
to make love. It has been a number of weeks

since the argument about the property line and where
the new shed would go. The girls are forbidden
to speak with one another. But that's another story,
one we won't be able to get to tonight. Instead,

let's switch off the lamp and begin our wondering
about how the girls managed the difficult feat,
how they were able to unwind a line across that gulf
and how long its presence might remain a secret.

These questions take their place in the catechism of good
night. Is the door locked and the oven off? Has someone

let in the cat? One of the parents, I won't say which,
glances out the window, and she happens to notice
the string, and so now we have to wonder how
she'll use the information, and also how she'll react
when she sees the small, dark figure tiptoeing along
the wire, over the gardens toward her daughter's room.

AT 2 A.M.

there is moon enough still

to walk home by, though

that destination has grown hazy

with time and entropy.

What had been a country road

became a suburban artery

and is in no way historic

except in the way

those who live in a place

deceive themselves with the notion

that theirs is a landmark experience.

I take note of where markers

might be placed

had someone notable lived here:

on this spot he fell

from his Schwinn Stingray

attempting a wheelie, or here's

the place he stood with binoculars,

peering into spectacular

Beaver Flanagan's bedroom window.

At the lawn's corner, a metal pipe

driven in to show the property line

still there, right where

the FOR SALE sign had been staked.

The blinds are down in the room

that had been my parents'; nothing to see here,

and besides,

headlights are coming on,

skittish, nighttime creatures,

romantic lies

of moon and stars diminishing,

brightly lit against dark morning sky.

SUPERSTITION

Who has turned the jade elephant's
head from the door? That won't do

with a gunman still on the loose, herons
flapping too close to the house, so I turned

fire tongs for luck, cast table salt
into flames. I spent the whole night

pointing at the moon before I could fall
asleep, creamy light shining on my face.

But by morning, my OCD flared again.
I tapped my forehead three times, rapped

the doorframe: Father, Son, and Holy Ghost.
Mostly, I have it under control; most of the time,

I only do it once. When the third heart
attack killed my father, I knew it was a liar.

I could finally let up. All that dread
had no place, and the wound seemed to heal.

My father died doing what he'd been told
not to do. He fell to the snow he'd cleared

from his car; he died on a mattress of snow.
Not even the scar I'd scored into my chest

with a silver crucifix had the power to save him.
When the snow melted and dried, I swept

dust from the spot into an envelope. Mom
sold the house and moved away. Years later,

I mixed that dust with flour and baked
coarse bread. I put some on my tongue and let it

dissolve. I swallowed with wine and waited,
fixed the elephant's green head toward the door.

BOURBON, CIGARETTES, VAN MORRISON

—Lake Anna, Virginia

The wind's picked up, rattling
half-dead leaves, snapping
off acorns that clatter through
branches and thud to the ground.
Wasps circle the screened-in porch,
probe corners, and the sky's
brief flirtation with blue

has passed behind the gray shade
drawn over hills beyond the lake's far shore.
Every now and then, a gust catches
the ceiling fan's wicker paddles,
and they turn, slowly. It's nearly too
obvious: Autumn begins in beauty
and ends with a cold rainstorm

in late November, too dismal
to mean anything else but winter.
I'd forgotten how music can shift
a body into depression like this, how
memory clings like cigarette smoke
to a damp sweater. And rain
begins drilling at the roof. Van

Morrison's given way to only
that percussion, whiskey's
flame in my belly. My mother
no longer speaks, but she grins
horribly at the nursing home,

flicks spit those days when she
fails to recognize me. The wasps

have given up. Eventually, so does the rain.

YOUR DAYDREAMING CHILD

Aren't you mad when the note comes
home from school? You have a problem
child. Instead of finishing math or science,

he's wasting time. Aren't you so damned
angry that you yell and threaten? Scream,
"Why the hell can't you just pay attention?"

But your child is completely at attention,
fully present and dealing with the fear
that his left arm is longer than his right.

He's trying so hard to make them even.
Under the desk, he's sticking himself
with a pin, or struggling to force the tips

of his index and middle fingers to line up.
Try it yourself—try to push your index
finger forward, out of its socket. Keep at it.

If you manage, maybe it's true that an arm
can be stretched into compliance. He knows
the teacher's glaring at him, that the period

is almost over, and so the period is almost
over ritual kicks in, the spiral notebook's
edge lined up with the rim of the desktop,

three Ticonderoga pencils back to back,
#2s in their ovals, each eased one quarter
turn toward the wall clock to push along

the minute hand. It's been going on like this
for months. Now, in exactly three minutes
before the bell goes off, he has to count

the cursive letters of the alphabet taped
above the chalkboard—A for Apple, one;
B for Balloon, two; C for Canary, three. It is

his own kind of math, but he can never get it
to add up. It's the dreaded new math
with which you both must now contend.

You must open the book and learn it together.

OCD

At least he's not undergoing an exorcism,
not being made to repent a litany of sins

that don't exist; at least well-meaning
Freudians aren't sticking their noses

into his toilet training, aren't picking at
the scabs of the divorce, though Danny

picks at his own scabs to make them bleed.
At least we know he can't help it, hasn't

volunteered to suffer blood, the digging
at his gums, the tics and pledges to remain

always true to this video game or that ball
python, the constant checking. He's done

his schoolwork poorly again and Christy
is tired, frustrated, anyone could see,

but Danny has trouble with expressions
and body language: *Are you mad, mommy?*

Are you mad? When Danny's struggling
and lets me look him in the eyes, I can almost

see through them into the orbital frontal
cortex where his wiring is probably frayed,

where the monster lives, a monster that's
not a monster at all but a hiccup that keeps

the striatum from braking fear, from
dismissing it as irrational. I'm peeking in

on him now. He's playing his very favorite
video game, one where he gets to kill all

the zombies. The game's both escape and
obsession. He has a ritual to keep it pure.

Last night he couldn't stop asking Christy
if she loved him. He needed to make sure

(tap) make sure (tap) make sure (tap)

CAPE BRETON HIGHLANDS

It could have been a bear,
crack of a branch, snuffled
breath in Cape Breton

darkness. I jostled sparks
from the fire to keep what
was out there at bay, lay

the final limbs of sugar maple
onto embers. No one in earshot,
my wife and stepson sleep

while the tent billows a little
in whispering breeze
wafting over the lake. Earlier,

night nearly caught us
on the hiking trail; we'd lagged—
mother moose and three calves

grazing there. We'd stumbled
upon them, and she'd tilted
her head as if she had antlers,

a thousand pounds or more
of her hooved the ground.
Just throw a rock, let's go, Danny

complained, picked up a stone
the size of a golf ball. *No!*
I hissed, his fist disappearing

inside my own, my compromised
heart clenching in my chest. Coyote
howled a hundred yards away.

Both mothers fronted their children.
Gray sky had darkened to near black.
I began to cudgel the ground

with a thick branch, inched
ahead, Oh, Lord, until the moose
diverged from us and ambled away.

SHRINE

I was driving through
rural Delaware, & I'd

never seen it before,
someone present &

mourning at a roadside
memorial, middle-aged

woman in a housedress
kneeling on a sloped berm,

bent over a homemade
cross, spray of cut flowers

splayed beside her
on the scruffy grass.

It couldn't have been
a more beautiful day,

scrimshaw clouds
skimming through pale

blue sky like swimming
angels or sea creatures

too singular to name.
In the back of my mind,

for weeks, that lone woman
curating grief while big rigs

whined by. Grainy vacation
Polariods. Languid jellyfish,

their dangling tentacles, & other
vague, chimeric visitations.

HAPPY HOUR AT JOEY ROMA'S RESTAURANT AND BAR

The guy at the end of the bar,
who'd been drinking vodka martinis for two hours,
swiveled his stool as if making
a difficult decision and had just decided to act.
Bathroom break, I thought,
but he tottered onto the riser in the corner,
dropped his ass down on the bench, and
bent into the yellowing keyboard of the scarred piano
balanced near the edge. It doesn't matter
what he played; it could have been
any old standard, but the thing is,
his delicate interpretation, how
everyone stopped talking
to listen for five minutes or so before he collapsed
into a discordant heap,
and then how most looked away and resumed conversations,
ordered another round, twirled
spaghetti on a fork. It all seemed part of the act, nothing
to see here, and when in Roma's . . .

I've always wanted to be that stranger
who materializes in a bar, has a few
cocktails among locals, then sits down
before the altar of all sad melodies,
cracks his stiff knuckles and begins to play.
I fight the urge to go up and hug the man. He still
has a song, and there are so many other tragedies.

II.

THE WEEK AFTER VALENTINE'S DAY

How many Russell
Stover heart-shaped
   chocolate boxes
   interred in blue
      recycling barrels
      lining our streets,
         that sweetness
         gone already?

AFTER LISTENING TO THE WEATHER, I PULL INTO A BAR

Sometimes, miles from home, you find wings
just the way you like them. The beer
is cold and cheap; the bartender
doesn't care about you and things

you might say. These are small blessings:
a dive that takes you in this way,
comfortable enough to pay
you no mind until your lager
runs dry. Pool balls clack, a wager
is made, and you decide to pray

to the bones piled up on your plate,
thank them for what they've given you.
A local feeds a buck into
the jukebox and it's not late yet,

you think. It's a song you don't hate
from the nineties, full of pity
and regret. The tender shimmies,
putters with the liquor bottles.
Her body language won't prattle,
show those things you aren't meant to see.

In the parking lot,
you feel drizzle on your face,
just as predicted.

Soon it turns to rain.
Planted, still you fail to leave.
Trees begin to sway.

SINGLE LIFE WITH CARDINAL
AND AMERICAN GOLDFINCH

A bird I'd never seen ere, bright
yellow with a black cap, black flare
of wings, leapt free from the oak into light,

alit in a straggle of grass at the roadside's edge,
where a muddy-red cardinal was feeding solo.
Before long, they seemed blithely domestic, no wedge

severing their peace at the table. So,
forgive my conjecture of bliss, it was only
the birds were not lovers, the birds were just lonely.

THE TINIEST TOAD IN MOORE COUNTY, NC

catches my eye, hopping with great care
over the rough flagstone. Don't spook her,
I think: if a toad springs from your path,
death is sure to follow. Never turn out
a toad at the threshold: the worst luck
will follow for a year. Finding the creature
in your home, remove it to nature
with kindness, for witches possess them
as familiars. If you happen on a toad's dead body,
place it on an anthill until the flesh is eaten away.
Its bones that don't bob easy on water,
those you wrap in white linen and hang
in a corner to engender love. On a new moon,
if the bones float in a stream, they're charmed; slide
them into your pocket or hang them from your neck
ere the devil gets them first. Then you can witch,
it's said and won't be witched yourself. She leaps
from stone near the fake frog pond's edge,
where the real frog eyes her with desire
from his tenuous perch on a lily pad.
She nestles under a leaf to hide her nudity.
Here in the poet's garden, she promises me
her tiny bones one day, a kiss for my civility.

CHIMES

Swaying slowly under red honeysuckle,
I've chimed in long enough. I'm dangling
from the far edge of the gazebo not to gloat
but to warn; so cut the short string and lower
me down, stash me away in the cluttered tool shed.
Stuck in summer's forgetful stupor, what sorry
fool wants tinkley clatter, surreal cacophony
butter-knifing through the debilitating humidity,
short steel pipes and ceramics vibrating like industry
reciting at the failed cusp of nature, its steamy desire.
It's no more precious than the phony koi pond
and waterfall, three sad frogs floating amid
plastic lily pads, and no more natural than day care centers,
pale babies who grow to be cutters, juiced-up beef
cattle and arterial stents, but where do we draw the line?
Japanese maples in North Carolina glow brightly
scarlet as evening wanders carelessly into the garden,
envelops the birdhouse, unpainted and tinged silver
by weather, pale green by the lichens. And what to say
about us? You adore those nature shows on television.
You admire the sharks—so what have you learned?
Let's be unlike the disturbance of wind and sorrow,
the railing captivity songs of frogs. Close your eyes
and this water's falling sounds too regular to be real; now,
open them and tell me again that something's wrong.

HUMMINGBIRDS & EAGLES

The whir of hummingbird wings. First here,
then fluttering over the pond, the wall of pine,

afternoon sun's mirrored lazy flickering.
And the place where, just last weekend,

we watched an eagle stand with certainty
on the bank before dipping into a long pull

of water, before lifting over greenery
and disappearing, as eagles seem destined to do.

Hummingbirds are cantankerous creatures
at the feeder, taking time only to hover briefly,

tiny bodies flapping under their riveted heads,
bickering for position, fencing with long beaks,

then thrusting them into the well. Sometimes
we disappear—or so it seems—into the neuroses

of hummingbirds. We want the nectar, that's all
and, when it's gone, we apologize, my love, and fall

into making up. We drink deeply of it, approach
even the nobility of eagles. Hummingbirds

can fly backwards, sideways, hover up and down;
they wear wedding clothes the rest of their lives.

Fashioned from leftover feathers the gods
used to create other birds, their long tongues

bypass the bitter protections of flowers.
They bring good luck, so we offer them succor.

I hold the funnel in place while you pour sugar-
water, blood-red, into the feeder, steady

me as I stretch from the footstool
to hang it from a small hook under the eave.

I step down into waiting arms; you sink your talons
nearly to the bone, tell me that you'll never leave.

THE VENUS OF WILLENDORF

The figurine never had feet, can't
stand on its own. Carved from
limestone, her heavy breasts

drape a morbidly obese torso,
sag nearly to her belly button.
Ample flesh folds over her hip bones.

The artifact doesn't seem to mimic
pregnancy. It's not the only example
either; did Stone Age sculptors dig

the Rubenesque before the Rubenesque
was hip? So much for the Paleo diet.
She has no face, but the top of her head

is neatly textured so as to suggest . . . what?
Plaits? Ornate headdress? Made so
to act as an apparatus for masturbation

or some fertility ritual? Was she a queen
bee, fattened and stashed away while
her sisters remained skinny? Or was she

a curiosity, made incredible by disease?
The great detail of the head assures us
that a face certainly would have been possible.

AFTER ROBERT MOTHERWELL'S *TWO FIGURES*

She's let the landlord enter, whose snaggle
of metal teeth had plucked the glass peephole

from the door as if it was an eyeball.
His enormous beer belly violates

the portal, blots out everything except
a thin shaft of light filtering in from

the hallway window, where she's often paused
to consider flight in a gossamer

dress, slipped from the ochre wall behind her.
She'd launch herself out over the river,

before her own man returns from the bar
to discover she's stashed the rent money.

The super pushes; the lock falls in place.
She leans forward into what must be done.

NOCTURNE

for Christy

Last night a barred owl swept across the road,
plunged into the hillside, then ascended,
some rodent, its clock run out, in its beak.
The owl settled into the nearby crook
of an oak and consumed at its leisure.

For twenty minutes or so, it perched there,
the occasional swivel of its head
my way, pale face under a pale half-moon
sizing me up, near drunk at the railing.
Lord knows, it could have been the alcohol,

but I was at Mass, a kind of rapture.
Earlier, the roar, distorted road music—
bike after bike rolling through Eureka,
startling birds and the poets. I'd seen
two *Eat Pussy, Not Pavement* T-shirts in

the space of an hour. Born they are, but not
so wild as they dream to be: long, gray beards
flapping in the breeze, leather-clad women
clutching behind them, tanned arms wrapped around
prodigious midsections, pressed tight, keeping

their motors running. And now, all seems less
dire, pale face under pale half-moon, a fierce
plunging, keen desire and you so far
away for so long now. These spring leaves, owl
in their veiling, wet road shining below,

and I'm rapt at the edge of the railing.

III.

L'HOMME AU CHEVALET, 1942

after Georges Braque

Upon lowering another dull
still life from his easel,
he divined a symbol in the tool;
his art, sad brushstrokes of a fool.

GREAT AGAIN: A SUITE

1.

GREAT AGAIN

7/4/18, Southern Pines, North Carolina

A hummingbird just visited
the porch, attracted, perhaps,
by my red beer cozy, or maybe

she's the raven at the window
this morning, shapeshifted now
to remind me of change. A cherry

bomb explodes beyond the trees;
a bullfrog bellows prematurely.
On another day, I'd have thought—

gunshot. It's the first thing
that goes through everyone's mind.
Another unarmed black body,

bullet hole in the back.
Everyone's mind
polluted with noise. And now,

another blast, hollow
point, disturbing the peace. My father
hated the 4th of July. He'd escaped

communists in Romania, was born
into war. If you want fireworks,
he'd say, go join the army. He loved

his new country, but it was hard
labor he believed in most, his
American Dream for us. He worked

himself to death. It's taken me 57 years
to feel this bullseye's growth, like wings,
dead between my shoulder blades.

2.

BIRD RIFF

Rancor lilies clamor in the White House Garden.
Gardener maddened, birds frighten
and take to the wing.

                        Tasting freedom
again, Noah's dove never returned.

                        Birds,

emboldened now, taunt from nearby trees,
squawk into microphones and shit on
the windowpanes. Birds

have hollow bones; that's why flight is a fragile
miracle, held aloft by faith and science, and birds,
descended from dinosaurs, are creatures of instinct: not

smart but wary. Millions of birds are killed
each year by domestic and feral cats

or shredded in wind turbines.
                        Three women
are killed each day by domestic violence in the U.S.

                        Some birds are

immigrants who come and go through fluid borders. If left
alone, they are beautiful while they're here. Hummingbirds

squabble and fence
with their beaks over red-dyed sugar water poured into feeders.
They hover, I assume, near lilies in the garden of the White House.

They've mistaken all the blood for food.

We've given Donald
a BB gun as a gift. We've told him to go out and play. Put out your eye,

Donald, then put out the other.   Thousands of songbirds
are killed each year by careless children.   A murmuration

of starlings shifts as one body in flight. The swirl
confuses owls and hawks; when the sun
goes down, they roost together in a safe patch of trees.

I love the audacity of birds,
braving larger tormenters, chasing them from their nests.

A Stone Age vulture-

bone flute is likely the oldest musical instrument. Researchers guess
music helped humans communicate and form tight social bonds—air
blown through a vulture bone or its trilling from the throats of wrens.

For some
indigenous Americans, eagle-bone flutes are sacred objects,
used for sun dancing, praying and healing.

I love the audacity
of birds, braving tormenters and chasing them
from their nests. The mobbing call is delivered,

and they cooperate, harass predators to protect their young. Nestlings
leap free of their moss-woven vantage points and into faith

and science. When you see a dead bird on the roadside, spit
on it so you don't get it for supper. When you hear a bird
thud against glass, cringe and await death

in the family. A swallow flew down the chimney and circled
the room three times before I thought
to open the front door and encourage him out.

                          The sun dance

was prohibited by immigrant settlers. Indigenous people
weren't allowed to openly practice the ceremony again

until the late 1970s, after a period of high profile activism,
including legal challenges to those laws. Noah's

                    dove never returned

after the third flight, but after the second,
when the dove alit onto his hand in the evening,
there in its beak was a freshly plucked olive leaf. Listen

to the mockingbird, still singing where the weeping willows wave.

3.

SOUTHERN PINES, JULY 2019

A bat flickers by, marking dusk's
rise of mosquitoes. A jet drags
its double trail through a pale sky,
then it fades away, leaving one
pinpoint star out over the long
leaf pines. Eerily quiet night
before the 4th day of July.
F. Scott Fitzgerald, Thomas Wolfe,
Sherwood Anderson and others
watched these trees turn from green to black.
Fitzgerald had hit his midlife
slump and would never recover.
In a year or so, Zelda would
be confined in Asheville. It was
1935; everyone
was depressed. F. Scott and Paul Boyd
distracted themselves with gossip
of Elva Statler Davidson's
mysterious death in Pinehurst.
Fortunate servants looked on.
In Germany, Hitler founded
the Luftwaffe. Der Führer was
two years into his dictatorship.
Donner and blitzen soon would pump
fear into the minds of children.
In the U.S., we'd develop
the bat bomb, a canister full
of Chiroptera armed with small
incendiary devices

clipped to their vampiric bodies.
In New Mexico, during trials,
bats were accidentally released and
torched the testing range to the ground.
They were supposed to pay back Japan
for Pearl Harbor, but I digress.
More bats have assembled, echo-
locating and zeroing in.

4.

THE NATURE OF NATURE

A bluebird shows itself, disappears
beyond tall pines, then reappears

in the bright golden company of Lesser
Goldfinch, big colors against summer

greenery. Be bold but small, they insist,
and quick to the wing because difference

is dangerous in America, no matter
how well you sing. Now one, now two,

now three turkey vultures circle the air
above, and that's not a welcome omen.

The bumblebee buzzing my colorful
beer can—a Belgian Tripel—is only confused

for a moment, climbs, then jets for the bed
of blazing star, their spikes of tiny

pink flowers. Elephant ears, lining
the brick wall behind the lily pond, are

eavesdropping and will never forget
my candor here without you. Even they feel

injured, and the bullfrog bellows, registers
his own complaints: Why me? Why me?

Three years ago today, I sat here, same
spot, Trump two years in, and heard

stray fireworks that led me to think
of gunshots, that brought me to remember

my father, that brings me to consider Danny,
riddled with his own collateral damage,

and you, Christy, and the frazzled state
of our union. I ask Colocasia; they always

remember. His illness threatens
with the bulk of a pachyderm. Weymouth

is beautifully curated and reminds me
of privilege. A black-chinned hummingbird

darts past, jabs awhile at purple blooms
in a pot. He jerks his head, swivels, flits

closer, stops, flits once more, stops hard
and hovers—twelve inches from my face—

to address me with kindness. Then he repairs
to his supper while tandemed cardinals—

one the muddy color of dried blood, the other
vivid blood-red—forage, young lovers there

among the manicured shrubbery. Be bold
but small, quick to the wing. Bang!

Cherry bomb in the distance. I've killed
so many birds, thoughtless kid with a pellet rifle,

I don't know why they show me such grace.
They forget, I think, or forgive, while

I've neither forgiven nor forgotten,
keep mercy dead in my crosshairs. Bang!

A flurry shudders the white hydrangeas.

5.

CURRENT EVENTS

From a folding chair, just inside
the rolled-up garage door, the moon

a day from full this Good Friday,
my view is scored by longleaf pine

needles, impatient in the breeze.
The stretched-out limb of the Japanese

Magnolia alongside our driveway sags
toward the top of my aging Toyota, lower

each season: even the blossoms seem
to weigh it down. Later this year, maybe

next, I'll have to saw it off. The world
is wary, unsure of what's to come.

Our children are awakened, but because
we don't trust them at all, we hover

and call that salvation, pass
desperate bills and laws, waylay

what's inevitable in the name of Jesus Christ
himself. So be it. This, too, is pealing bells

lost in currents of time, each
desperate pull of the rope hanging

an awful burden by its neck.
See it there, up in the branches,

something that looks human kicking until
it's only ghost nerves and evening wind.

I stub out my cigarette. The stone
is so heavy. We'll need a miracle to budge it.

IV.

EUREKA SPRINGS

circa 1879

After the miracle, we returned to our lives,
that difficult labor rebuilding the village
one stone at a time. It wasn't as we'd arrived.
Tempted by lore, we didn't see it as pillage,

how we left no place on earth free of our steps. Yes,
enticed by the magnetic power of the springs,
the promise of a cure for advancing blindness,
we staked pale tents, seemingly remnants of white clouds

dropped from the blue skies fair weather brings, curious
blessings. But it was trickster, and the shapeshifting
began. Those rags begot cabins; nefarious
winds blew; skies darkened, the pall of hucksters drifting.

This new vision was just sightlessness reinscribed.
After the miracle, we returned to our lives.

ONE WEEK BEFORE THE SOLSTICE

12/14/2020

I went to the local market
to pick up a few holiday
things: a rosemary topiary

shaped like a Christmas tree,
a chocolate Santa for Danny,
a bag of mixed nuts, maybe,

to crack in front of the fire
with Christy. Disguised, I dodged
masked strangers, remembered—

a miracle!—gluten-free gravy
and three lemons. The Electoral College
confirmed Joe Biden today;

the orange monster bound for
one hell or another, but in the nursing
home, my mother wastes away

into a Covid New Year. Tomorrow,
I'll arrange for a virtual appearance.
Her room has a sizeable window, so

I hope for a flurry while we ZOOM.
She's lost speech, and her mind
may as well be a nostalgic snow globe.

With a slight jerk of her head,
she'll conjure a beautiful landscape—
captive and captivating—sifting

in stray beams of remembered sunlight.
An Amazon van rumbles through
the cul-de-sac. I plug in the colored lights.

Rosemary graces the air faintly
with pine. Hazelnuts, walnuts, almonds
and pecans fill the festive bowl.

Sally, the neighbor's Border Collie,
begins to bark, and I'm grateful
to be alone tonight. I'm filigreed

ice, flimsy on the glittering surface
of Pablo's metal water dish: short-lived,
fragile as mom's whisper in winter dark.

TO THE BONE

Amherst, Virginia, 1/21/2022

The Blue Ridge Mountains are cobalt
blue today, almost unnaturally so,
wrapped around the frozen distance.
Such a beautiful obstacle,
hazing the air with isoprene

giving this range its color,
accounting for one third
of all hydrocarbons released
into the atmosphere. It's hard to

argue with the appropriateness
of such blue in our time. A married
pair of cardinals offer the only other
hues against drab gray, posted
there in bare branches to bear witness,

to whistle our story of mutual doom
into the wind. Yesterday's slush cracks
under my shoes, and my mother's ashes
are stored on a shelf in New York,

waiting. We are waiting together
for the appropriate blue, convenient
day—my sisters and I—to slide
her into a Ferncliff mausoleum
drawer next to our father, who's

had to wait to lie with his wife once more.
This is the story as my own body
begins humming its winter song. How cold it is
outside, everything at the point of breaking.

GROTTO SPRING

Eureka Springs, Arkansas, 5/1/22

Glint of some creature's eye in Ozark lightning,
robust redolence of April from the earth,
all things preparing for rain in Ozark lightning.

For an hour, I've sat by the gurgle of Grotto Spring,
drift of myrrh turning it holy, her death
in the glint of some creature's eye in Ozark lightning.

For an hour, I've prayed in my manner, sky darkling,
ensconced and rapt here in the hollow's breath,
all things preparing for rain in Ozark lightning,

almighty electrical pulsing, erratic flickering,
and some skittish creature giving me wide berth,
the alarmed glint of its eye in Ozark lightning.

At sunrise, a hummingbird, metallic green at the deck's railing,
had cocked its head—the glint of its tiny eye. I lapsed into great depth
as all things prepared for evening's rain and Ozark lightning.

To see the depth of her dementia was devastating.
I severed free of that pain and gave it wide berth,
and now a discerning eye in burgeoning lightning—
crackle of thunder—taking my measure, quivering lightning.

MY SECOND SPRING

It's said, if a man witnesses,
in a single year, a second
spring, he pays with a season from
his life. Thousands of miles away,

thanks to this new climate's largesse,
summer has already begun.
Fledglings peer from the lips of nests.
Behold the huge, peculiar world

into which each bird will tumble.
Gray squirrels gambol and flirt below.
Our spent azalea blossoms rot
into soil. Let it be winter

I relinquish, if it must be
early death. My father's plummet
into a snowbank he'd shoveled,
how his heart gave out in the cold.

His only instruction was not
to be set into frozen earth.
I saw his smoke, therefore, sifting
through March, strokes from that gray palette.
Amen, then, it's winter I'll forfeit.

JESUS. FRANKENSTEIN. DANNY'S MONSTERS.

An Ozark lightning storm flickers
the night sky like a black-and-white

movie, like Victor Frankenstein's
laboratory. Thunder rumbles

through the mountains. The breeze kicks up
and again it begins to rain,

again, a flood warning startles
my cellphone. I don't know what I

can say about his ambition,
his sin of conjuring a new

life free of sin. I don't buy that,
of course, sin is an acquired

talent, but what might appear sin
at arm's length, behavior that seems,

from one's safe distance, ungodly,
perhaps diabolical, is

sometimes an original weight,
genetic imbalance, a sin

of god, if sin must be ascribed.
I think sometimes how my stepson,

in less enlightened times, would have
been exorcised. It's that simple.

Ticcing of Tourette's, OCD,
the inability to read

facial expressions and self-harm—
the kid wouldn't have had a chance.

He might not have a prayer still,
as far as enlightenment goes.

We've no fear of holy water,
the Bible, beads or crucifix.

Those tools of the trade we can keep
at arm's length. It's not the clergy

keeping us up at night. Frankenstein
wanted to father a being

without defects, but the monster
was stitched together with human

parts, so quickly learned of human
sin, how it feels to be shunned by

even one's creator. I can't
help but sympathize with Victor.

The synoptic Gospels credit
Jesus for the exorcism

of a demonically possessed,
moonstruck boy, foaming at the mouth

and unwilling to speak. *How much
longer must I be among you?*

Jesus asked the crowd. A *faithless
generation*, he christened them

before the boy's father explained
that the child's suffering began

at birth. It was epilepsy,
we know now, no demon at all.

Jesus Christ, then, was a doctor,
not an exorcist; this detracts

not at all from the miracle.
I believe; help my unbelief,

the man had begged, and so would you
in similar circumstances.

Again, that flashing of lightning,
again, I'm in the lab, ready

to pull any damn switch, confront
any damn god blocking my way.

That's what I choose to believe, sure.
Another boom shakes the window,

more pelting rain. Later, Jesus
revealed to the disciples why

they'd failed in their attempts to cure
the boy: *This kind,* said the savior,

can come out only through prayer.
How much longer, he asked, *must I*

be among you? As if he had
something better to do than heal

the sick. The electricity
has failed. I light beeswax candles

to keep the child's monsters at bay.
I should don my purple hoodie

and take a long walk in the rain.
Such sacrilege. And miracles.

And no sane place to keep our grief.
I believe; help my unbelief.

CHANT

A leaf wafting into solemn
monophony, Gregorian

chanting melody drifting here
in the room. I want to lay down

those parts of my heart that have died
in the hollow of the copper

beech and beseech the queen fairy
to tell me what's next. It was hard

shoving the splinter into my thumb
so that I might carry it

for luck into the world to come.
Chants are intoned in unison,

one note simultaneously.
All singers enliven the same

melody. If only Congress
could attend with such discipline

and intent. Someone's created
a snow sculpture on the fence post,

and it's melting in the sun while
the Red-faced Warbler examines,

voices his interpretation.
And now the birdfeeder's agog.

I can feel the splinter throbbing.
Kyrie Eleison, have mercy.

ONE AMONG MILLIONS,

a snowflake, yearning for earth,
lands on my warm tongue.

MITCHELVILLE, SOUTH CAROLINA

In memorium, Toni Morrison
2/18/31–8/5/2019

In my head, I can't help but hear
the stomp and shuffle, clap and joy

of Christmas Eve into Christmas Day.
Draped over live oak limbs, Spanish

moss resembles the gray beards of elders:
its resilience, how it assimilates nutrients

solely from air, trapping water
and particulates, silver garland

tossing its seed to the winds
to survive. For the Mitchelville

freedmen, perhaps it offered
solace as they stepped from

the Praise House, fatigue and holiness,
emergent joy only such dedication

to purpose can conjure. Ghost
notes sound the morning mist.

The salt marsh surrounds
Fish Haul Creek, just below

Port Royal Plantation where
"contrabands" would be enslaved.

Toni, from your Bench by the Road,
I look out over marsh grass, gray

span of water in the distance,
almost indistinguishable

from sky but for one
thin band of pale blue

and, therein, the dark outline
of a passing kayaker. I envision

him one of the chosen, casting
a hand-fashioned net from his bateau,

the process unchanged from biblical times,
skill passed from grandfathers

and fathers, each net begun
with 36 eyes tied together

with 18,000 knots, 200 hours
of labor to create meshwork

with a five-foot circumference.
Some slaves escaped into the confusion

of the Battle of Port Royal Sound,
others were just left behind. As in the

aftermath of a hurricane, their owners
later returned to see what property

could be salvaged after naval ships
and guns disappeared. In the end,

it wasn't much of a fight. Each 12 x 12
shotgun house had its ¼ acre for farming

greens and sweet potatoes. Toni,
there's something in the tortured

limbs of older trees that have
withstood too many storms. The last

time I sat here, only two years ago,
this bench seemed not so weathered.

Now it appears tethered between spirit
and flesh, shackles and levitation.

Groups of vacationers, all white
and Covid-distanced, stroll by to visit

the end of the dock. I don't think
they know what this is. Beloved,

there was a window, ten minutes
maybe, when it was all silence.

Soon elders appeared, faint clapping,
stomp and shuffle, counterclockwise

circle, song and praise, haunted chants
the prayer house can't hold. They ringed

the building—traversing time, turning
to pure spirit before me. They

lifted as one toward the ether, and
even Jesus there to usher

toward hush, the rarely seen Clapper
Rail calling, riding this cloudy sky.

NOTES

The Garcia/Hunter epigraph: The epigraph is quoted from the lyrics to "Uncle John's Band," the first track on the Grateful Dead's album, *Workingman's Dead*.

"The Venus of Willendorf": *Venus of Willendorf*, c. 24,000-22,000 B.C.E., limestone 11.1 cm high (Naturhistorisches Museum Vienna). According to *Britannica.com*, "It has been suggested that she is a fertility figure, a good-luck totem, a mother goddess symbol, or an aphrodisiac made by men for the appreciation of men. Further, one researcher hypothesized that it was made by a woman and that '[w]hat has been seen as evidence of obesity or adiposity is actually the foreshortening effect of self-inspection.'"

"Mitchelville, South Carolina": The Bench by the Road Project is a memorial history and community outreach initiative of the Toni Morrison Society. The Project was launched on February 18, 2006, on the occasion of Toni Morrison's 75th Birthday. One of these benches is located in Mitchelville, South Carolina.

According to *Wikipedia*, Mitchelville was a town built during the American Civil War for formerly enslaved people, located on what is now Hilton Head Island. Named for local Union Army general, Ormsby M. Mitchel, the town was a population center for the enterprise known as the Port Royal Experiment, a program begun during the American Civil War in which former slaves successfully worked on the land abandoned by planters. "The town or village continued relatively intact into the early 1870s. But sometime in the early 1880s, Mitchelville . . . dissolved to a small, kinship-based community that survived into the 1920s. A 1920 topographic map of Hilton Head Island shows a cluster of buildings centered around a church. Previous archaeological investigations have concluded that the majority of Mitchelville was abandoned by c. 1890."